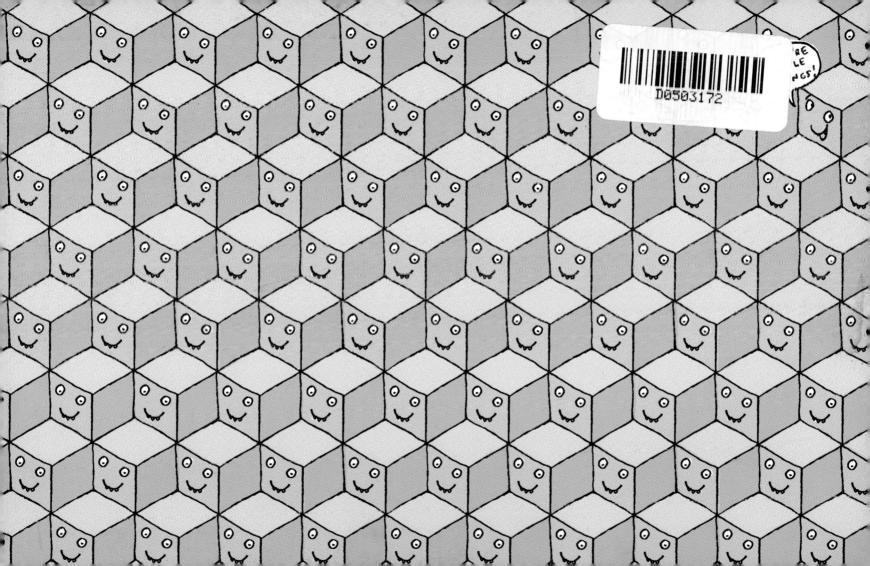

For Martin J. and the whale-sized teleosts
N. D.

For little, tiny Erica Lavender
N. L.

First U.S. edition 2009

Library of Congress Cataloging-in-Publication Data is available.

Library of Congress Catalog Card Number 2008938394

ISBN 978-0-7636-3924-2

10 9 8 7 6 5 4 3 2 1

Printed in China

This book was typeset in AT Arta.
The illustrations were done in ink and digitally colored.

Candlewick Press
99 Dover Street
Somerville, Massachusetts 02144

visit us at www.candlewick.com

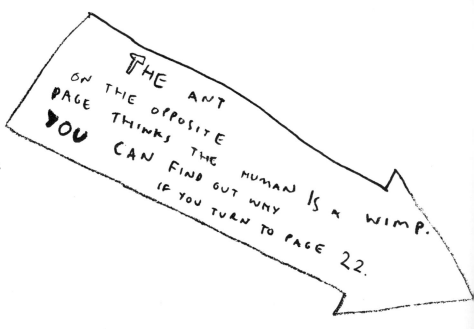

THE ANT ON THE OPPOSITE PAGE THINKS THE HUMAN IS A WIMP. YOU CAN FIND OUT WHY IF YOU TURN TO PAGE 22.

Just the Right Size

Why Big Animals Are Big and Little Animals Are Little

Nicola Davies

illustrated by **Neal Layton**

CANDLEWICK PRESS

In comics and movies, superheroes zoom across the sky,

run up walls, lift things as big as buses, and

use their powers to fight giant monsters!

It's all very exciting, but it's a complete load of nonsense.
Real humans can't fly, hang from the ceiling,
or even lift things much bigger than themselves . . .
and real giant animals couldn't exist, since they
wouldn't be able to walk or breathe.

In fact, there are very strict rules that control what bodies can and can't do. These rules keep
creatures from getting too big, and because of them, the *real* superheroes are usually small—a lot
smaller than humans.

Meet Some Small Superheroes and Real Giants

Teeny **hummingbirds** and tiny **wasps** are the nimblest fliers on Earth.

Geckos no bigger than your hand can walk up walls or on ceilings.

Leaf-cutter ants are only ¼ inch long and weigh less than ³/₁₀ of an ounce, but can lift many times their own weight.

Rhinoceros beetles can carry 850 times their own weight.

The world's largest ape, the male **gorilla** is teeny compared to King Kong. At 5 feet 6 inches tall, he's probably just about as tall as your dad!

YOUR DAD

MALE GORILLA

KING KONG'S FOOT

12 inches

The biggest spider on Earth, the *Lasiodora* **spider** is only 12 inches long—about the size of a dinner plate.

Rules Against Super Powers

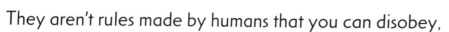

So what *are* these rules that stop us from having super powers?

They aren't rules made by humans that you can disobey,
like "no ice cream before you eat your broccoli" or "no parking here." Instead, they are rules that are part of the way our universe is put together. You can't get around rules like "light travels in straight lines" or "things on Earth fall downward when you drop them." The rules that mean giant apes exist only in movies and Superman isn't real (sorry!) are rules of geometry—which is the kind of math that's about size and shape.

WOOF!

LITTLE THING

The best way to explain these rules is to take a close look at the difference between little things and big things.

Here is Little Thing. It could be anything—a car, a log, a bar of soap—but it just happens to be a creature (even if it looks a bit like a cube).

Let's take a few measurements of Little Thing, such as . . .

Now let's meet Big Thing.
Big Thing is TWICE the size of Little Thing (that is, Big Thing is twice as long, twice as wide, and twice as tall as Little Thing).

How many Little Things would it take to make one Big Thing? (Remember, Big Thing is twice as long as Little Thing.)

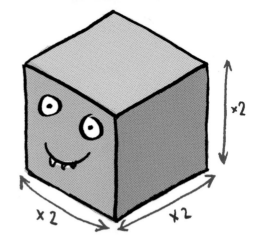

×2

×2 ×2

Two Little Things together look like this:

Four Little Things isn't enough either:

It takes EIGHT Little Things to make one Big Thing!

If you look carefully, you can see that Big Thing's surface area and cross section are FOUR times bigger than Little Thing's. But Big Thing's volume and weight are EIGHT times bigger.

This rule—let's call it the Big Thing, Little Thing rule, or BTLT for short—works on animals and plants and people and anything:

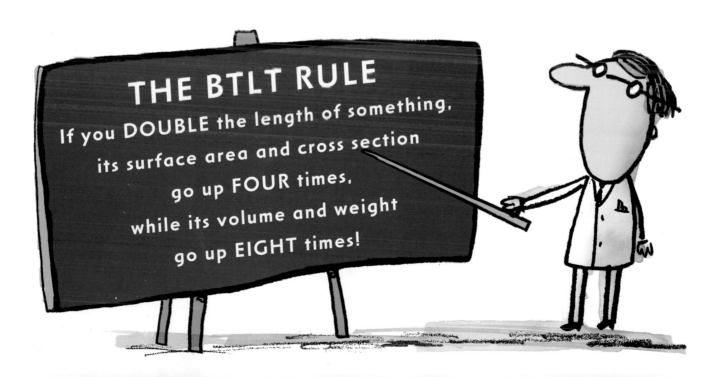

THE BTLT RULE
If you DOUBLE the length of something,
its surface area and cross section
go up FOUR times,
while its volume and weight
go up EIGHT times!

The BTLT Rule — Alive!

The BTLT rule isn't just about numbers, though: it has a big effect on how living bodies work. Some important features of bodies—like how much food and air they need—depend on volume and weight. Others—like the strength of muscles—depend on cross section or surface area.

It's easy to see that Big Thing is going to need as much food to eat and air to breathe as EIGHT Little Things. But if we take a slice through Big Thing, we can see that its muscles are only FOUR times thicker than Little Thing's muscles . . . making it only four times stronger.

14

The BTLT rule makes some things quite impossible for bodies to do or be! It stops monsters such as car-sized spiders from existing in the real world, and it also means that humans can't lift buses and could never flap their arms and fly.

4 TIMES thicker than this

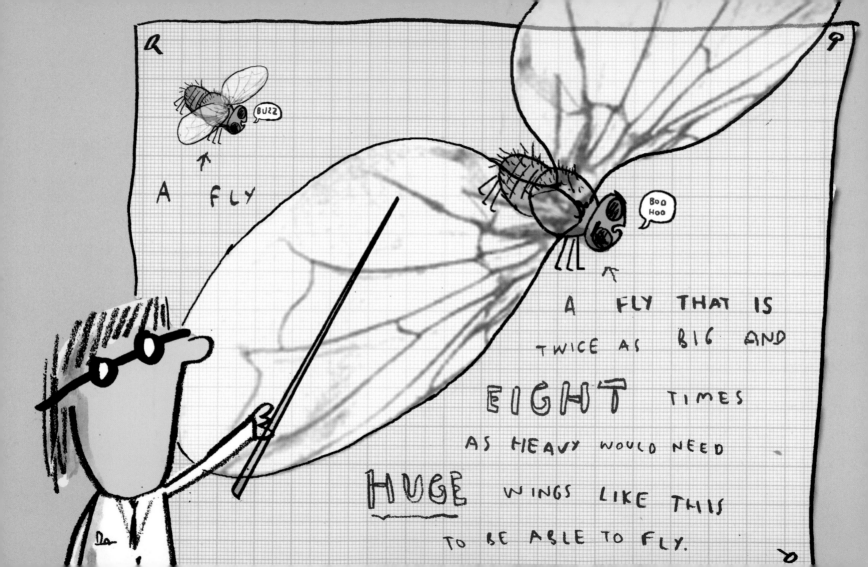

Why Humans Can't Take Off

For the very teeniest fliers, such as insects as small as one of these letters, takeoff is easy. A puff of wind on their wings is enough to get them airborne. But because of the BTLT rule, flying gets harder the bigger you get.

If you could take an insect and make it twice as big, its outside (or surface area) would get four times bigger, which means its wings would also get four times bigger. Its muscles, too, would be four times thicker and so four times as strong (muscle strength depends on cross section—remember?). This would be fine if the insect were just four times heavier, but because of the BTLT rule, it would weigh EIGHT times more. So it wouldn't be able to take off unless its wings and its muscles were much, much bigger.

This is why heavier insects, like dragonflies, need very big wings to get them off the ground, and birds need huge chest muscles and large, feather-covered wings.

But wings and muscles can't keep up with heavier and heavier bodies. That's why really big birds like ostriches and emus can't fly and walk instead, and why the only way humans can fly is with the help of engines.

PHUT
PHUT

17

Dancing on Water

Look at the surface of a pond on a summer's day and you'll see insects called water striders perform the amazing feat of walking on water. So how come they can do it and we can't?

Water has a kind of thin skin on its surface where all the tiny particles that make up the water line up. It's called the surface tension, and it's what the water striders walk on. They spread their weight using long, skinny feet, like skates, so that they don't press too hard and push through the surface tension.

But if water striders were twice as long, the weight those feet would have to hold up would be eight times bigger (remember the BTLT rule?), and their feet would need to be eight times longer—too long to move, in fact!

That's why you don't see animals bigger than water striders—such as humans—dancing on top of the water: they would need ridiculously large feet!

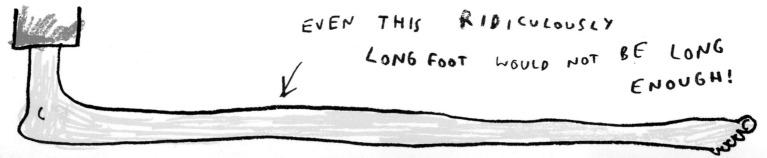

EVEN THIS RIDICULOUSLY LONG FOOT WOULD NOT BE LONG ENOUGH!

Walking on the Ceiling

It's a similar story with walking on the ceiling. Spider-Man does it, but in real life the biggest ceiling-walkers are lizards called geckos. They hunt insects on the ceiling and can even run up panes of glass.

The secret's in their toes, which are shaped like flattened spoons. Under a microscope you can see that gecko toes are covered with thousands of tiny hairs. These hairs can fit tightly onto the smoothest wall; so tightly that the microscopic forces that hold the tiny particles of the wall together hold on to the hairs, sticking them fast. Adding up the stickiness acting on so many hairs gives enough sticking power to keep the gecko on the ceiling.

21

So why can't we have spoon-shaped "hairy toes" and run up walls like a gecko? The answer (of course!) lies in the BTLT rule. We weigh thousands of times more than a tiny gecko, and we'd need toes tens of thousands of times bigger than a gecko's to hold us on the ceiling—much too big for running around without tripping!

EVEN HAIRY TOES THIS BIG WOULD NOT BE BIG ENOUGH!

Why We Can't Lift Buses

An ordinary ant can lift between ten and fifty times its own weight, and a rhinoceros beetle can carry 850 times its own weight on its back. Yet the best human weight lifters can lift only about four or five times their own body weight. How can little insects be stronger than big humans? It's the BTLT rule at work again.

On the opposite page is Little Thing. Let's say Little Thing can lift something as heavy as itself.

Also on the opposite page is Big Thing. Because muscle strength depends on cross section, Big Thing is FOUR times stronger than Little Thing, so Big Thing can lift four times as much as Little Thing.

But because Big Thing weighs the same as EIGHT Little Things, Big Thing can't lift something as heavy as itself. It can lift only something *half* as heavy as itself.

That's how ants can be stronger than humans!

Getting Rid of Monsters

I'm sorry if you are disappointed to hear that you will never be able to fly, sprint up windows, dance on ponds, or be stronger than an ant. But since you can't be a superhero, the BTLT rule will do your monster-busting for you. Let me show you how. Let's start with a Terrible Tale of Giants. . . .

Once upon a time there was a giant who was just like a normal human, only ten times bigger all over: ten times taller, wider, and deeper, making him one thousand times heavier. The giant took his first giant step, and with a giant crashing sound, both his legs snapped. The end. (And exactly the same thing happened to the giant's best friend, the monster spider!)

Remember, strength doesn't keep up with weight, because strength depends on the size of the cross section. In this case, the cross section, or slice, through the giant's leg is a hundred times bigger than a normal human's, so only a hundred times stronger— much too weak to take the giant's huge weight, a thousand times greater than a normal human's!

A real 60-foot-tall giant would need legs that were so thick they would probably be too heavy to lift.

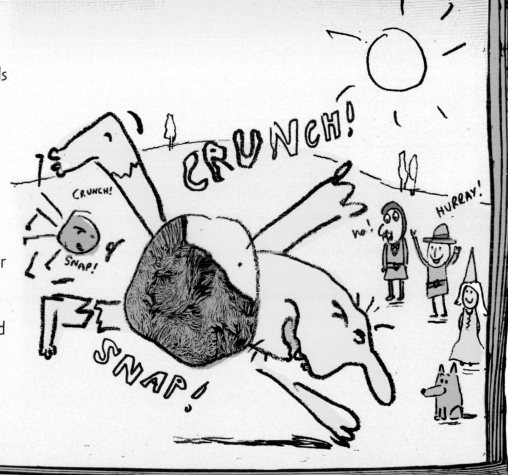

Big, Bigger, Biggest?

Legs can't keep getting thicker to hold up bigger and bigger animals, because thick legs are heavy to move. Scientists think that this is what put an upper limit on the size of dinosaurs. The biggest dinosaur was 120 feet long and weighed 100 tons. Any heavier and it would have needed legs too thick to move.

So it's not surprising that the heaviest animal that has ever lived doesn't need legs at all. The blue whale can be 100 feet long and weigh up to 190 tons—but since its weight is supported by seawater, why can't it be even bigger than that?

A double-sized, 200-foot blue whale would have eight times the body volume of a 100-foot whale: its gut would need to digest eight times more food, its lungs would need to breathe eight times more air, and its kidneys would need to get rid of eight times more pee than a 100-foot whale. But internal organs get bigger with the area of a whale's cross section, so they'd be only four times larger than in a 100-foot whale. Thus, a double-sized blue whale would need guts, lungs, and kidneys so big that they wouldn't fit in its body.

This probably explains why the biggest blue whale ever found was just 110 feet long.

AN ARTIST'S impression OF
Planet Earth 4,000,000,000 years ago....
A TINY SIMPLE CREATURE
A BIGGER SIMPLE CREATURE
A MUCH BIGGER SIMPLER CREATURE...
Aghh! CAN'T BREATHE.

Rules on the Inside

As you can see from the story of the blue whale, the BTLT rule works on the insides of bodies as well as the outsides. It's been doing that since the start of life on Earth and it's had a big effect on how living things evolved, from simple to complicated.

Life on Earth first started (almost four billion years ago) with little creatures so small it would take more than fifty, laid end to end, to cross the period at the end of this sentence. They were really, reeeeeally simple—just one cell big with no mouth, guts, or lungs. They didn't even have to breathe: they just floated around in the water, and the oxygen they needed could drift in through their skin. That's because they had quite a big surface area and a small volume—in other words, a lot of skin for not much body.

If such a creature were to double in size, it would have four times more surface area but eight times more volume. That means it would need eight times as much oxygen but would have only four times as much skin to get it through. If it went on getting bigger, pretty soon it would have too much body and not enough skin to get its oxygen through.

This is why simple, single-celled creatures can't get very big. To get big, living things had to get complicated.

Folds and Wrinkles

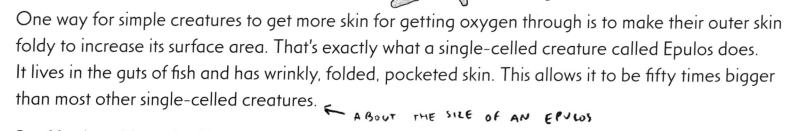

← A CLOSE-UP OF SOME EPULOS

One way for simple creatures to get more skin for getting oxygen through is to make their outer skin foldy to increase its surface area. That's exactly what a single-celled creature called Epulos does. It lives in the guts of fish and has wrinkly, folded, pocketed skin. This allows it to be fifty times bigger than most other single-celled creatures.

← ABOUT THE SIZE OF AN EPULOS

But fifty times bigger is still only the size of a period, and having your whole outside covered in crinkly skin gets in the way of having useful things like legs and heads. So bigger animals, made of many many millions of single cells (each human is made of around 100 trillion cells), have found that it's better to have all your foldy skin for getting oxygen in one place.

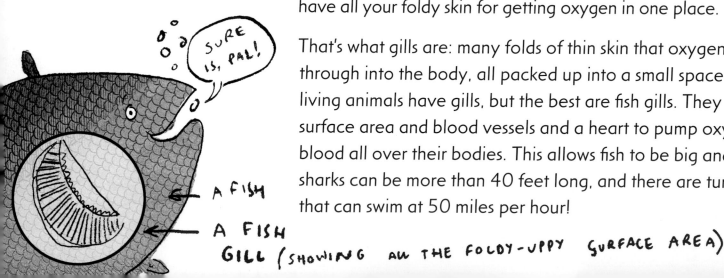

SURE IS, PAL!

← A FISH

→ A FISH GILL (SHOWING ALL THE FOLDY-UPPY SURFACE AREA)

That's what gills are: many folds of thin skin that oxygen can pass through into the body, all packed up into a small space. Most water-living animals have gills, but the best are fish gills. They have a BIG surface area and blood vessels and a heart to pump oxygen-carrying blood all over their bodies. This allows fish to be big and fast: whale sharks can be more than 40 feet long, and there are tuna and marlin that can swim at 50 miles per hour!

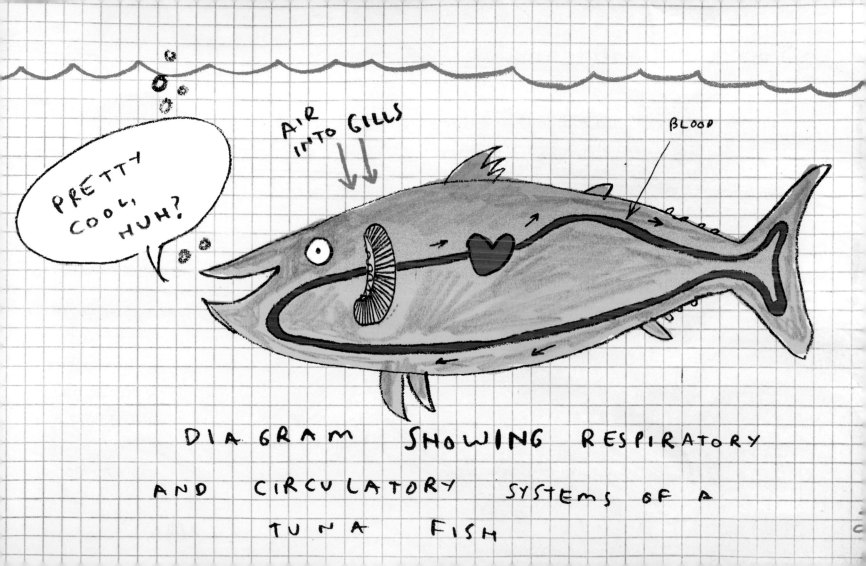

Books and Tubes

Gills are fine in water, but they have to stay moist to work, and on land they shrivel up in the dry air. So when animals started to live on land, they had to evolve other ways to have lots of moist skin to get their oxygen through.

Spiders have "book lungs," skin folded like the pages of a book, inside air-filled pockets in their tummies. The book lungs work fine until a spider has to run more than a few dozen feet. Then they don't work well enough to keep the spider's brain and muscles supplied with oxygen, and the spider just faints. (So two things make giant spiders impossible: snapped legs *and* fainting.)

Insects have a maze of little tubes, called tracheae, leading from holes, called spiracles, on the outside of their bodies to deep inside. The deepest tubes are very tiny and lined with thin skin that lets oxygen through to the blood. If the tracheae were longer than about half an inch, not enough air would make it to the bottom of the tubes. With air coming in from spiracles on both sides of their bodies, insects can be twice as wide as the longest tracheae — but no wider. Even the biggest insect in the world, the African goliath beetle, with a body 5 inches long, is little more than an inch wide.

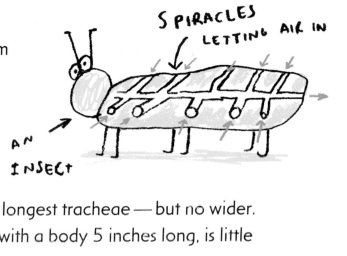

33

Get Big with Lungs

← A FAT BEETLE

If spiders and insects had been the only animals around, there might never have been anything bigger on land than a fat beetle. But around 400 million years ago, some fish evolved simple lungs that allowed them to swim at the surface and breathe air. This made it possible for the first amphibians to evolve and crawl out onto dry land.

34

Lungs started out as simple bags, but over millions of years, they got more and more complicated to give a bigger and bigger surface area for getting oxygen. The hearts and blood vessels that worked with them got better too. Mammal lungs are some of the most complicated of all. They are spongy bags, made of millions of tiny air sacs, to give a really HUGE area of thin skin for breathing. (If you spread all the tiny air sacs that make up your lungs out flat, they would cover most of a tennis court!) Mammal hearts are super-efficient. They pump blood fast, delivering oxygen to every cell in a network of minute blood vessels. (If all the little blood vessels from your body were laid end to end, they would reach halfway to the moon!)

Together, lungs and improved hearts allowed animals on land to evolve into lots of different kinds—reptiles and birds and mammals.

The moon ↓

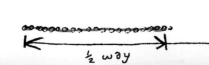

½ way

Want to be BIG?! Then you NEED these...
THE ALL-NEW, IMPROVED MAMMAL LUNGS!
SUPER-EFFICIENT MAMMAL HEART!
GASP!

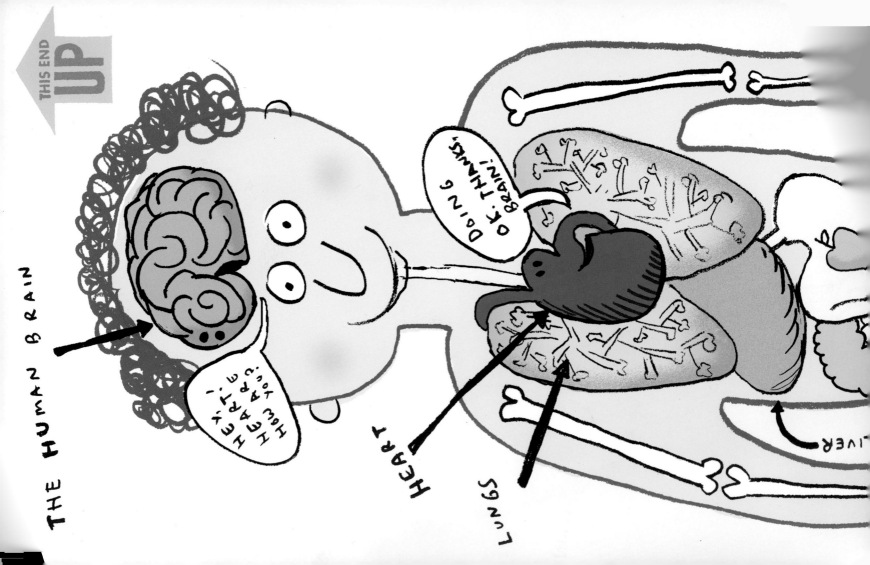

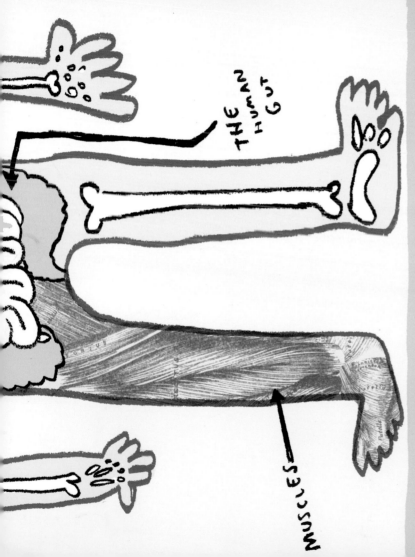

THE HUMAN GUT

MUSCLES

Big and Complicated

A simple, single-celled animal just soaks up food and gets rid of waste the same way it gets oxygen—through its skin. But as we've seen, the BTLT rule makes that impossible for bigger animals. So, to do those jobs, bigger animals have internal organs that, just like lungs and gills, pack a huge surface area into a small space.

The lining of the human gut, for example, is folded into millions of tiny fingers that would cover 3,000 square feet (more than one and a half tennis courts, if it were spread out flat). What's more, all those clever internal organs have to communicate so that they can work together to keep the body healthy.

Thanks to the BTLT rule, the insides of bodies have evolved into very complicated places.

It's Tough Being Tiny

All in all, getting big seems like an awful lot of trouble. Why not stay small and simple, like those first animals? In fact, many creatures do just that. Bacteria are very similar to those first little life forms, and they are everywhere (there are ten times more of them living in your body than your body has cells).

The main problem with being so small and simple is that it's very dangerous. All sorts of little accidents—like a gust of wind, a shower of rain, or an afternoon of hot sun—can wipe out billions of tiny bacteria. They are too small to travel far or fast enough to get out of trouble, and for them, the air seems as thick as soup, and water as sticky as syrup.

There are lots of mouths around that are big enough to swallow them too, and since eyes and brains need many millions of cells to work, they don't have any way of seeing a predator coming or figuring out what to do about it. It's tough being tiny.

39

The Not-So-Super Superheroes

Bigger, more complicated animals like insects can avoid some of the problems of the super-teeny, super-simple creatures.

They can travel to escape danger and to find food; they have senses to warn them of danger; their brains, though pretty small, can help to solve basic problems; and, as we've seen, they can perform like superheroes. But they still suffer a host of perils just because of their small size.

The BTLT rule allows them to lift huge weights and zip around on the surface of a pond, but it also means that they have a big surface area for their tiny volume. For animals this small, just getting wet can be fatal. The film of water around a wet, ant-sized body can weigh many times more than the ant does, making it hard for small animals to move when they get soaked. What's more, the surface tension of the water acts like a wrapping of stretchy cellophane, trapping the animal inside, so it may even drown!

This is why insects are very careful when they take a drink. They usually do it through long, strawlike mouth parts so that there's no risk of any other bit of body getting wet.

Cold-Sized

A LABRADOR DOG → ← A COMMERSON'S DOLPHIN

Small animals have a bigger outer surface area for their volume than big animals, so they have trouble keeping warm when it's cold; their body heat just leaks out through their skin. This is a real problem for mammals, who can die from cold.

Being small is even more of a problem in water, because water is better than air at taking body heat away—think of how freezing you can get in the pool! So one of the smallest mammals that lives all its life in the water is the Labrador retriever-sized Commerson's dolphin. (Mouse-sized or even rabbit-sized dolphins would cool down too fast.) Commerson's dolphins keep warm by eating a lot—about 11 pounds of fish and squid every day — and by having very good insulation: a thick layer of fat under the skin.

43

There are plenty of smaller mammals and birds that visit water to find food — tiny water shrews, as small as your finger, and little penguins not much larger than a carton of milk, for example—but they couldn't survive the heat-stealing cold full-time.

PART-TIMERS!

TINY WATER SHREW

LITTLE PENGUIN

Hot Dinos

Mammals that live full-time in water are mostly a lot bigger than the Commerson's dolphin, because big bodies hold on to their heat better. But being big and warm has other benefits for other sorts of animals too; in fact, it may have been the secret of the dinosaurs' success.

Reptiles, like snakes, lizards, and crocodiles, are all cold-blooded. That means they bask in the sun to soak up heat through their skin to get their bodies warm enough to work. But when the sun goes down and it gets cold, the skin that got them warm loses heat just as fast, and they cool down — and a cool reptile is a sluggish reptile. The smaller the reptile, the worse it is, because smaller reptiles have bigger skins (surface area) for their volume.

Dinosaurs were reptiles too, but the big ones had a much smaller surface area of skin for their volume than smaller modern reptiles. So once they warmed up, they held on to their heat. Many scientists now believe that this allowed bigger dinosaurs to keep warm almost all the time, and if they were warm, they could be active.

So it could be the BTLT rule that made *Tyrannosaurus rex* into a fearsome predator!

Cheap Flights for Small Fliers

The world's champion travelers, though, aren't big.
They're Arctic terns. These little birds, not much
bigger than sparrows, travel 20,000 miles every year from the Arctic to the Antarctic and back
again. That's farther than any other creature on the planet!

They can do it because flying, especially for something as light as a tern, is "cheap"—it uses very
little food for every mile traveled. It's like having a car that will go 5,000 miles on a gallon of gas.
Arctic terns stock up on food before they start traveling and put on fat that
will fuel them for thousands of miles.

Swimming, walking, and running use far more food per mile, so on land and
in the water, long journeys are possible only for the biggest walkers and
swimmers, who need less food for their size than littler animals.

Biggest Winners

There are advantages to being big that have nothing to do with surface area or with the sort of food an animal can eat. The bigger you are, the fewer predators there are that can make you into their dinner, and the bigger you are, the more fights you can win.

In elephants, the males, or bulls, fight like mad over who mates with the females. The biggest bulls with the biggest tusks are the most successful, which is why male elephants are so much bigger than females.

It's the same for sperm whales, where males can be almost twice as big as the females. In fact, in almost any species where there are fights over females, males are bigger, even if it's just their horns or their tails.

Size differences that don't seem very noticeable to humans really matter to female animals and birds. Female swallows much prefer to mate with males whose tail feathers are longer . . . even if it's only by fractions of an inch. And female frogs and toads can tell big males from little ones even in the dark, because the big ones say "ribbet" in a deeper voice.

Big Voice — Little Voice

Bigness isn't always for fighting and showing off; it can be good for communication too. Blue whales keep in touch with one another over huge distances by making deep humming sounds. Only the deepest hums can travel the hundreds of miles to another blue whale, and only very, very big animals can make very low-pitched sounds.

Being huge helps blue whales keep in touch, but being small helps bats find their way in the dark: they squeak, then listen to the echoes of their voices to get a sound-picture of all that's around them. Low-pitched squeaks would give a very fuzzy sound-picture, so bats use very high-pitched sounds, which give them detailed echo-pictures. And only very teeny little vocal chords can make those high squeaks.

55

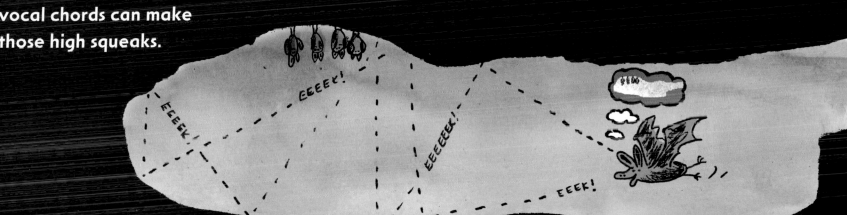

Big AND Small

So being small isn't always a bad thing (just remember the smallest superheroes at the start of the book). Small animals like mice or bats may be snack-sized, but because they are tiny, there are lots of places for them to hide. Small animals don't need much space or food, so there are many ways that they can make a living. A tiger might need a whole forest as its habitat, but a beetle would be happy with a hole in a log.

In fact, there can be so many good things about being small that some species that were once big have evolved back into something smaller. Once upon a time gibbons were large, tree-climbing apes, more like chimps. But when they started to get around in the forest by swinging from branch to branch by their arms, having a nice, light little body was very useful. So over time, they got smaller. Now gibbons are the smallest of all the apes and can weigh as little as a fat domestic cat.

Just the Right Size

Being the right size is one of the ways that living things can adapt to where they live. *Tiny* is the best bet if where you live is between two grains of sand, but *huge* might be better if your habitat is the whole ocean. So animals and plants come in a mind-boggling range of sizes: the biggest, the blue whale, is 1,000,000,000,000,000,000,000 times bigger than the smallest microbe.

But if it weren't for the BTLT rule, size might be almost the only difference between all these living things. Earth might be populated by creatures that looked like different-sized blobs: little ones living under stones and between grains of sand, medium ones blobbing about on land, and huge ones in the sea. Without the BTLT rule, there would be no need for complicated bodies: single-celled blobs of different sizes would do just fine.

To obey the BTLT rule, living things evolved that weren't just different sizes but different shapes and patterns too. This has resulted in all sorts of bodies: bodies with one cell or millions, with bones or shells, with gills or lungs, with legs or no legs; bodies that can be "superheroes" and bodies that can think about why they can't be. An ever-changing kaleidescope of life, a glorious diversity of species, from the very tiniest to the most enormous—and all of them . . .

Index

Glossary

cells tiny units, too small to see, from which all living bodies are made

cross section the surface you would see if you sliced through the middle of an object

geometry the set of rules that explain the shape and size of objects

gills lots of folds of thin skin found on either side of a fish's head. They take in oxygen from the water and pass it into the bloodstream.

gut a long soft tube (also called an intestine) where food gets digested. Almost all animals have a gut folded up in their belly.

lungs squishy bags with lots of tiny pockets inside that fill with air when an animal breathes, so that oxygen can pass through the thin skin of the pockets into the blood

mammals animals with warm blood and fur that feed their babies on their own milk: Mice, elephants, kangaroos, bats, and humans are all mammals.

oxygen a gas that all living creatures need in their bodies to make them work. Animals and insects get it from the air. Fish get it from water.

particles very tiny pieces that make up a larger thing. Some things (like water) are made of just one type of particle, but most things (like bodies) are made up of lots of different types of particles.

surface area how big the outside of something is

surface tension a sort of skin that forms on the top of water, where the particles are packed very closely together

61